Animal Neighbours

Otter

Michael Leach

WAYLAND

Animal Neighbours

Titles in this series:

Badger • Deer • Fox • Hare • Hedgehog • Otter

Conceived and produced for Hodder Wayland by

Nutshell
MEDIA

Intergen House, 65–67 Westerm Road, Hove BN3 2JQ UK
www.nutshellmedialtd.co.uk

Commissioning Editor: Vicky Brooker
Editor: Polly Goodman
Designer: Tim Mayer
Illustrator: Jackie Harland
Consultant: Paul Yoxon, International Otter Survival Fund

Published in Great Britain in 2003 by Hodder Wayland, an imprint of Hodder Children's Books.

This paperback edition published in 2007 by Wayland, an imprint of Hachette Children's Books.

British Library Cataloguing in Publication Data
Leach, Michael, 1954–
Otter. – (Animal neighbours)
1. Otters – Juvenile literature
I. Title
599.7'692

ISBN-13: 978 0 7502 5085 6

Printed and bound in China.

Wayland,
an imprint of Hachette Children's Books
338 Euston Road, London NW1 3BH

Cover photograph: An otter sniffs the air for signs of danger.
Title page: After a long night's hunting, an otter falls fast asleep on a grassy river bank.

Picture acknowledgements
Ecoscene 24 (Chinch Gryniewicz); FLPA 7 (Gerard Laci), 11 (E. & D. Hosking), 13 (S. Charlie Brown), 25 (P. Reynolds), 27 (Foto Natura Stock), 28 right (S. Charlie Brown); Michael Leach 6; NHPA *Cover* (Andy Rouse), *Title page* (Alan Williams), 8 (Joe Blossom), 10 (Laurie Campbell), 12 (Stephen Dalton), 14 (Bill Coster), 15 (Laurie Campbell), 16 (Andy Rouse), 17 (Agence Nature), 19 (Andy Rouse), 20 (Henry Ausloos), 21 (Alan Williams), 22 (Laurie Campbell), 23 (Michael Leach), 26 (Andy Rouse), 28 top (Joe Blossom), 28 bottom (Laurie Campbell), 29 left (Michael Leach); OSF 9 (Paul Taylor).

Contents

Meet the Otter

Otters are semi-aquatic members of the weasel family. They live on coasts, and beside rivers, lakes and marshes.

There are 13 species of otter alive today. They live on every continent, apart from Australia and Antarctica. This book looks at the European otter, the most widespread species.

▲ **The red shading on this map shows where otters live in the world today.**

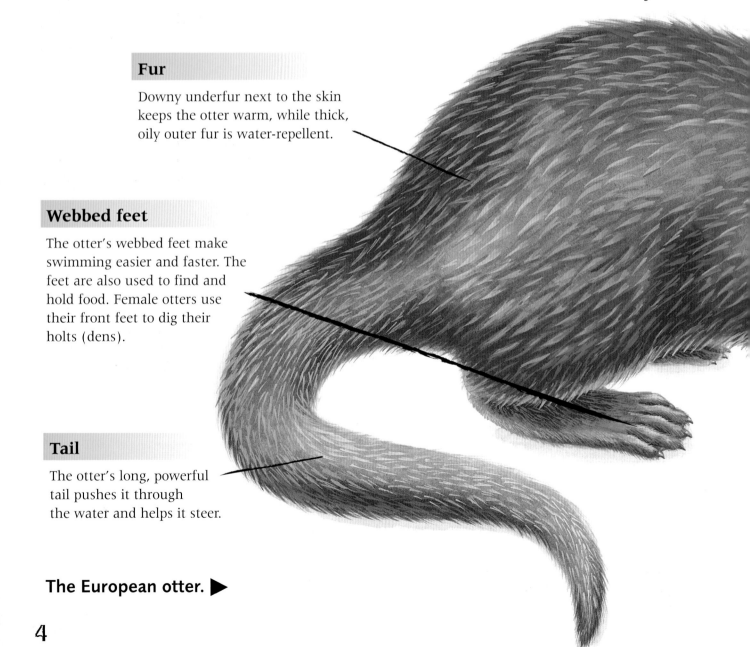

Fur

Downy underfur next to the skin keeps the otter warm, while thick, oily outer fur is water-repellent.

Webbed feet

The otter's webbed feet make swimming easier and faster. The feet are also used to find and hold food. Female otters use their front feet to dig their holts (dens).

Tail

The otter's long, powerful tail pushes it through the water and helps it steer.

The European otter. ▶

4

◀ The otter is a third bigger than a domestic cat.

Ears

Otters have excellent hearing on land. Their ears close automatically when they swim underwater.

Eyes

Otters can detect movement very well over long distances, both on land and underwater. Their eyes are forward-facing, ideal for spotting prey.

Nostrils

On land, otters have an excellent sense of smell. Like their ears, their nostrils close automatically when they swim underwater.

Teeth

Long, sharp front teeth catch and hold slippery fish. The back teeth are strong and flat for chewing.

Whiskers

Long, sensitive whiskers help the otter to hunt underwater. The whiskers sense movement underwater, which helps the otter find fish, especially at night or in muddy conditions when it is difficult to see.

The Weasel Family

There are 67 members of the weasel family, including badgers, stoats, skunks and polecats. All members of this family have long bodies and short legs. They are all predators, but they are shy animals that are usually found in quiet areas, well away from towns and cities.

Otters are often mistaken for mink. However, mink are much smaller than otters. Mink and otters are the only members of the weasel family that are semi-aquatic.

▼ The wolverine is one of the largest members of the weasel family. It is a powerful hunter that lives in northern Europe and North America.

SMALLEST OTTER

The Asian short-clawed otter is the smallest member of the otter family. It is just 90 cm long. Its front feet have only a little webbing between the toes, which means it is able to use its claws as hands, turning over rocks and plants to look for prey.

▲ An Asian short-clawed otter stands up on its hind legs to get a better view of any predators.

The pine marten is a close cousin of the otter that lives in forests. It is a predator that hunts small mice and voles on the ground, but also climbs high in the tree-tops searching for squirrels.

The largest otter is the giant otter. It is about 1.8 metres long. The heaviest otter is the sea otter, which weighs about 45 kilograms. Sea otters were almost wiped out by over-hunting in the nineteenth century. Today their population has grown to more than 100,000 animals.

Birth and Growing Up

Otter cubs are born in a den called a holt. This can be under rocks or among tree roots, but it is usually very close to water. The holt is lined with grass and moss to make a soft bed for the new-born cubs.

At birth, otter cubs are blind and toothless. Their mother spends a lot of time with them at first, suckling the cubs several times a day. She only leaves the holt to find food for herself. If the holt is disturbed by people, animals or even another otter, the mother will move the litter to a new site, picking up the cubs in her mouth and carrying them one by one.

▲ At 10 weeks old this otter is still fluffy. It has not yet grown the long, oily hairs of an adult.

OTTER CUBS

New-born otter cubs are about 15 cm long and weigh about 40 g.

The cubs are born covered in fine, fluffy hair. As they grow, this fine hair is gradually replaced by thicker, oily fur, which makes the otters buoyant in the water.

There may be up to five cubs in a litter, but the average size is two or three.

▲ An otter cub pauses at the holt entrance to sniff the air for danger.

The cubs start to crawl when they are about 5 weeks old. This is also the time when their eyes start to open. At about 7 weeks, the cubs eat their first solid food, which is fish brought back to them by their mother. At first, the cubs sniff at the fish, unsure of how to eat it. But they quickly learn and are soon fighting for their share.

Early days

The cubs suckle their mother's milk until they are about 14 weeks old. This is also the age when they first enter the water. At first the cubs are very afraid of the water and their mother often has to drag them in. She will grab them by the scruff of the neck and pull them into the water. Once they can swim confidently, the cubs follow their mother on hunting trips and learn how to find food.

▲ A female otter leads her two cubs across the seaweed on a Scottish beach, looking for food.

In these early weeks, the cubs play for several hours a day, chasing each other and play fighting, both on land and in the water. Playing teaches the cubs how to stalk and pounce on prey. It also strengthens their muscles ready for the time when they must kill their own food.

▼ Otters play in the water by rolling, diving and hitting each other with their front feet.

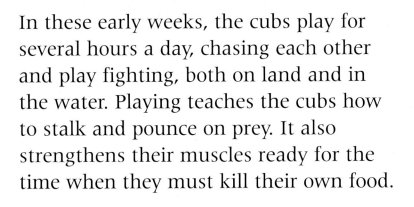

OTTER-SKIN CLOTHES

For several centuries in Europe and North America, otter cubs, especially the cubs of sea otters, were hunted for their soft, waterproof fur. This was made into hats, trousers and other clothes, which were sold for high prices. In the nineteenth century alone, thousands of otter cubs were killed for their fur. During the twentieth century, otter hunting was gradually banned in most countries, although the American river otter is still hunted in the USA and Canada.

▲ The entrance to an otter holt is often near water. The entrance slopes upwards, so the den inside stays dry.

Habitat

Young otters stay with their mother until they are about a year old, when it is time to find their own territory. This must be an area close to a river, lake, marsh or the coast, where they can hunt fish, their most important food.

Otters can only win their own territory when they are big enough to fight off rivals. At first they wander from place to place, being driven off by larger otters defending their own territories. As they come across a new suitable area, the otters are careful to smell the

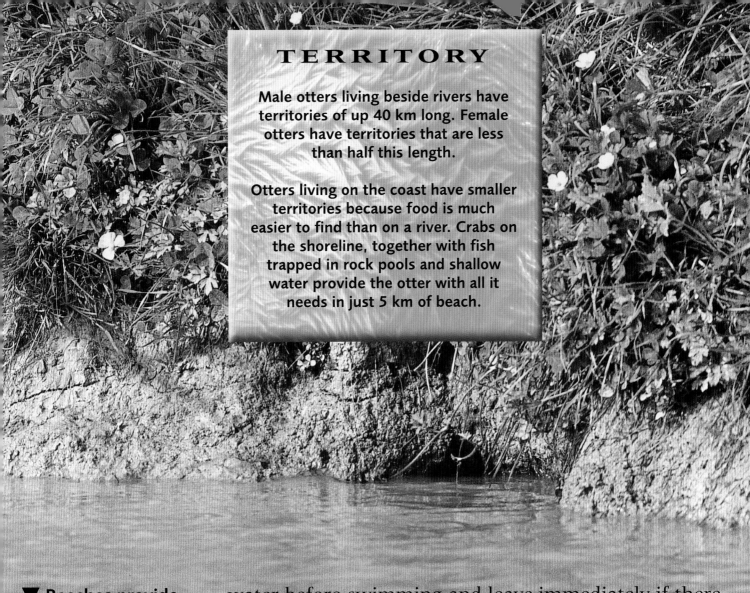

TERRITORY

Male otters living beside rivers have territories of up 40 km long. Female otters have territories that are less than half this length.

Otters living on the coast have smaller territories because food is much easier to find than on a river. Crabs on the shoreline, together with fish trapped in rock pools and shallow water provide the otter with all it needs in just 5 km of beach.

▼ Beaches provide lots of fish for hungry otters.

water before swimming and leave immediately if there is a strong scent of chemicals or oil. Polluted water can poison otters and the fish that they eat.

The strongest otters win the best territories. These contain the richest feeding sites and are the least disturbed by people. Once an otter has found a good territory, it usually stays there for life. Weaker otters, who are not strong enough to win their own territory, will wander from place to place for a while. But if they do not find somewhere suitable, eventually they will die. About 50 per cent of young otters die in their first winter.

Competition and fighting

Adult otters are solitary animals. They keep away from each other apart from at breeding times, so fights are not common. Males do not compete with females for living space, so it is possible for two or three females to live in the same territory as one male. Fighting only happens when an animal of the same sex moves into the territory of another, or when a female rejects the advances of a male.

▼ Otters use their long canine teeth as weapons when fighting rivals.

▲ Otter spraints are often the only clues that otters are around.

When two males meet in the same territory, their arguments are usually a display of strength rather than violence. Each male grunts, growls and shows his teeth while staring into the eyes of his rival. The weaker animal usually backs down quickly and leaves to avoid injury.

SPRAINTS

Otters constantly mark their territory with droppings left on rocks or high mounds of soil. These are known as 'spraints'. They are used as scent signals, to tell other otters that the territory is already taken. If an otter smells the droppings of a stranger in its territory, it will follow the scent and drive off the intruder. By sniffing another otter's droppings, an otter can find out its sex and how long ago it passed by.

Fighting only breaks out when the two otters are evenly matched in both size and strength. Even then, the battles are short and one male usually runs off before it is injured.

Land and water

Otters are well-suited to life both in and out of the water. On land, they move with a light, bounding trot and can easily outrun a human over short distances. In water, the otter's long, supple body is perfectly streamlined for slipping gracefully through the water. Its thick, outer fur acts as a barrier to stop its downy, underfur becoming wet, which is essential to prevent the otter getting cold.

▼ Otters have long, flexible backs that provide extra power when running or swimming.

OTTER CALLS

Otters use a wide range of calls to communicate:
- Adults make a long, loud whistling cry.
- Cubs make short chattering calls.
- A low growl is a sign of being frightened.
- A sharp bark shows anger.
- A low twitter is a sign of being friendly.

▲ Air trapped inside the otter's thick fur is forced out during a dive. This trail of bubbles can easily be seen on the surface of the water.

Otters swim in one of two ways. One method involves flicking the back half of their body in a powerful up-and-down movement, kicking their hind feet while keeping their front legs close to their chest. Otters also swim in a type of 'doggy-paddle', using all four legs independently.

Otters have an amazing ability to instantly turn and dive when swimming at full speed. They can completely change direction in a fraction of a second, which is a useful skill when hunting fish.

Food

Otters are carnivores. They feed mainly on fish, but because they spend time on land and in the water, they also eat a wide variety of other animals. Crabs, frogs, birds, and small mammals such as water voles and even rats are all part of the otter's diet.

▼ The otter is at the top of its food chain. Here are some of the animals that otters eat. (The illustrations are not to scale.)

Otter food chain

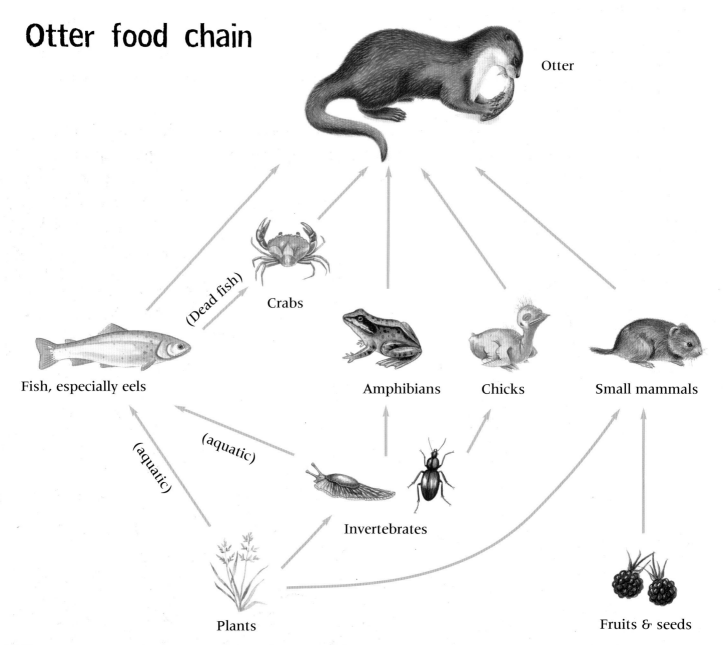

Otter

(Dead fish)

Crabs

Fish, especially eels

Amphibians

Chicks

Small mammals

(aquatic)

(aquatic)

Invertebrates

Plants

Fruits & seeds

The otter's diet changes throughout the year, depending on the food available. In the spring, frogs are easy prey for otters when they gather together in huge numbers to mate and lay spawn. The spring is also a good time to find nests of young birds or voles, which otters discover using their sense of smell.

Fish numbers do not change much during the year so in winter, when other food is scarce, this is the bulk of the otter's diet.

▼ Adult otters eat about 1 kilogram of food a day to help replace the energy used to hunt.

▲ Otters are not always successful hunters. Fish can move very quickly and many escape.

Hunting

River otters are usually nocturnal hunters. Each otter has its own favourite hunting site, which it visits every night. The nights are split between periods of high-speed hunting and eating, followed by periods of rest.

Otters have different hunting methods. In deep water they dart and dive, trying to grab passing fish with their long, sharp canine teeth. Sometimes they explore the riverbed by turning over stones with their nose, looking for animals beneath. The stiff whiskers on an otter's face are very sensitive to movement underwater. They help find fish swimming in muddy rivers and lakes, or at night when it is too dark to see. On river banks, otters use their excellent sense of smell to find voles and mice.

At dawn, the otter finally stops hunting and finds somewhere quiet to spend the day. This could be in a quiet hole in a river bank, or hidden amongst plants on the water's edge. Otters may even rest in large drainage pipes if there are no people nearby.

▼ After a long night's hunting, an otter falls fast asleep in the sunshine.

HUNTING TOOLS

Sea otters in the Pacific Ocean are among the very few animals to use tools for hunting. They gather shellfish from the seabed, then return to the water surface and float on their back. The otters open the shells by hitting them on a large rock balanced on their chests.

Finding a Mate

After the age of about 18 months, female otters are ready to breed. Males are not ready to breed until they are about 2 years old. They have to be strong enough to win their own territory before they can breed.

▼ **Dogs stay very close to bitches that are ready to mate.**

When a bitch is ready to mate, the scent of her droppings changes. This gives a sign to any dogs nearby, who regularly check the droppings of bitches. The dogs will follow the scent to find the bitch.

At first, the bitch may run away or even bite the dog, but eventually she allows him nearer. Over the next few days they mate many times, in water or on land. The pair may stay together for several weeks, but the dog usually leaves before the cubs are born.

The dog will move on to mate with several bitches and may father about 20 cubs during his lifetime. About 62 days after mating, the otter cubs are born.

▼ **This dog and bitch are about to mate.**

BREEDING TIMES

Most mammals have their young in the spring. During the summer, they can grow big enough to survive the cold winter months, when there is less food around. European otters are different. They will mate at any time and cubs can be born throughout the year. This is because fish numbers do not change much during the year, so there is always a reasonable food supply for the cubs.

Threats

Fully grown European otters have no natural predators. They can defend themselves against other carnivores, such as foxes and badgers, using their sharp teeth as powerful weapons. Smaller species of otter, such as the Asian short-clawed otter, face much bigger predators. They are sometimes hunted by crocodiles and even tigers.

▼ After the *Sea Empress* oil tanker ran aground off the coast of Wales, oil covered this beach and many others nearby.

The otter's most dangerous enemy is people. Otters living on coasts are at risk from oil spills, when an oil tanker suddenly spills its load. Oil spills cause great damage, killing all sea life for many kilometres around the site of the actual spill.

Fertilizers and ▶ pesticides are washed into rivers from surrounding farmland.

Water pollution is one of the otter's biggest threats. Chemicals from industrial waste and farmland are washed into rivers and seas every day. They pollute the water, poisoning otters and the fish that they eat. Fuel leaks from river and ocean traffic add to the water pollution.

Some otters are accidentally caught in underwater fishing nets, where they become trapped and drown. Others are illegally shot by landowners, who believe that otters are stealing their fish.

Breeding and conservation

During the twentieth century, the population of otters dropped dangerously low. In some countries, such as Austria, they became an endangered species. They have become extinct in Switzerland, Holland and Belgium. There are now projects in many countries to help save wild otters and stop them becoming extinct.

Some otters are specially bred in captivity and their cubs released into the wild. Before the cubs are released, their new habitat is carefully chosen.

▲ Conservationists build artificial holts for otters in areas where there are no natural holes to use.

The new habitat must provide clean water, plenty of food and be away from all disturbance. Artificial holts are often built, which give the cubs a safe shelter while they learn to explore their new surroundings.

Many cubs have survived since being released into the wild and now breed successfully. The population of European otters has slightly increased over the past 20 years, but the species is still threatened by human activities.

▼ The giant otter was once a common species, but the population is dropping because of illegal hunting.

ENDANGERED OTTERS

The European otter is an endangered species in most of Western Europe. Other threatened species are:

- Marine otter of Chile and Peru
- Giant otter of South America
- Southern river otter of South America
- Hairy-nosed otter of Thailand and Vietnam

Otter Life Cycle

1 The new-born otter cub is blind and weighs just 40 g. It is usually one of a litter of two to three cubs.

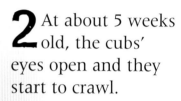

2 At about 5 weeks old, the cubs' eyes open and they start to crawl.

3 At about 7 weeks old the cubs eat their first solid food.

4 At about 16 weeks old the cubs join their mother on hunting trips.

5 The cubs leave their mother when they are about 1 year old.

6 After the age of 18 months, the otters mate and produce young.

Otter Clues

Look out for the following clues to help you find signs of an otter:

Holts

Holts are built beneath tree roots or large rocks, usually close to water. The area around the holt is well-trampled and often muddy. If there is mud or sand nearby, there should be footprints. It is very important not to disturb a holt if you find one. In many countries it is against the law.

Droppings

Fresh otter droppings are black, slimy and mound-shaped. After a few days the droppings turn white (see page 15). Fish-scales, bones and shells can often be seen in the droppings.

Each otter dropping is 3–10 cm long.

Footprints

A good footprint will clearly show the webs between the otter's toes. Otter footprints are very big and cannot be mistaken for those of any other animal. A walking otter leaves prints that are about 35 cm apart. When running the prints can be 90 cm apart.

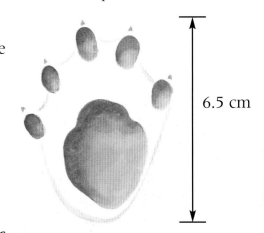

6.5 cm

Slides

Otters sometimes build slides down steep river banks. The slides are steep, muddy paths about 30 cm wide where the undergrowth is flattened or even ripped out. Otters seem to make slides for fun. They will often slide down a muddy bank into the water, climb out and do the whole thing again.

Food remains

Fish scales, fins and bones are signs of an otter's feeding site.

Flattened plants

An area of flattened plants with tracks leading to a river could be an otter's resting place.

Bubble trail

Otter fur contains a lot of air, so as an otter swims underwater, air is forced out and leaves a trail of bubbles on the surface (see page 17).

Glossary

bitch A female otter. The females of domestic dogs, foxes and wolves are also called bitches.

buoyant Able to float in water.

canine teeth Long, sharp teeth towards the front of the mouth that are used for killing prey and tearing meat.

carnivore An animal that eats meat.

dog A male otter. The males of domestic dogs, foxes and wolves are also called dogs.

endangered A species whose population is very low.

extinct No longer existing.

habitat The area where an animal or plant naturally lives.

holt An otter's den.

industrial waste Waste from factories, power stations or other industries.

invertebrates Animals that do not have a backbone.

litter A group of young animals born at the same time from the same mother.

nocturnal An animal that is active at night and sleeps during the day.

pollution Poisons, chemicals and other artificial substances that harm the environment.

predator An animal that kills and eats other animals.

prey An animal that is killed and eaten by other animals.

semi-aquatic Animals that live in water and on land.

solitary Animals that live alone.

spawn The eggs of fish and frogs.

spraints Otter droppings.

stalk To creep slowly and quietly towards prey, trying not to be seen.

suckle When a mother allows her young to drink milk from her teats.

territory An area that an animal defends against others of the same species.

water-repellent A surface that is difficult for water to pass through.

Finding Out More

Other books to read

Animal Sanctuary by John Bryant
(Open Gate Press, 1999)

Animal Young: Mammals by Rod Theodorou
(Heinemann, 2000)

Classification: Animal Kingdom by Kate Whyman
(Wayland, 2000)

The Giant Book of Creatures of the Night by Jim
Pipe (Watts, 1998)

Life Cycles: Cats and Other Mammals by Sally
Morgan (Chrysalis, 2003)

New Encyclopedia of Mammals by David
Macdonald (OUP, 2001)

Otters by Bobby Tulloch (Colin Baxter
Photography, 1999)

Otters on the Loose by Louis Dorfman (Windsor
House Publishing, 1998)

Sea Otters by Beth Wagner Brust (Wildlife
Education, 2000)

The Wayland Book of Common British Mammals
by Shirley Thompson (Wayland, 2000)

What's the Difference?: Mammals by Stephen
Savage (Wayland, 2002)

Wild Britain: Seashore by R. & L.
Spilsbury(Heinemann, 2002)

*Learning About Life Cycles: The Life Cycle of a
Bean, Cat, Chicken, Frog, Honeybee and Salmon*
All by Ruth Thomson (Wayland, 2006 &
2007)

Organisations to contact

Countryside Foundation for Education
PO Box 8, Hebden Bridge HX7 5YJ
www.countrysidefoundation.org.uk
Training and teaching materials to help people
understand the countryside and its problems.

International Otter Survival Fund (IOSF)
7, Black Park, Broadford, Isle of Skye IV49
9DE
www.otter.org
A conservation group that promotes the
protection of 13 species of otter worldwide.

The Mammal Society
2B Inworth Street,
London SW11 3EP
www.abdn.ac.uk/mammal/
Promotes the study and conservation of
British mammals.

The Otter Trust
Earsham, Bungay, Suffolk NR35 2AF
Tel. 01986 893470
www.ottertrust.org.uk
A conservation group that breeds and releases
the European otter into suitable places in
Britain and France. It has a junior members'
club and produces educational packs for
schools.

Wildlife Watch
National Office, The Kiln, Waterside,
Mather Road, Newark NG24 1WT
www.wildlifetrusts.org
Junior branch of the Wildlife Trusts, a network
of local Wildlife Trusts caring for nearly 2,500
nature reserves, from rugged coastline to urban
wildlife havens, protecting a huge number of
habitats and species.

Index

Page numbers in **bold** refer to a photograph or illustration.